marine
KNOTS

Originally published in France by Éditions Glénat under the title *Le b.a.ba des nœuds marins*.

Marine Knots. Copyright © 2016 by Glénat.
Translation copyright © 2018 by HarperCollins Publishers,

Text by Patrick Moreau

Illustrations by Jean-Benoît Héron

HarperCollins books may be purchased for educational, business, or sales promotional use. For information please email the Special Markets Department at SPsales@harpercollins.com.

Published in 2018 by
Harper Design
An Imprint of HarperCollinsPublishers
195 Broadway
New York, NY 10007
Tel: (212) 207-7000
Fax: (855) 746-6023

harperdesign@harpercollins.com
www.hc.com

Distributed throughout the world by
HarperCollins Publishers
195 Broadway
New York, NY 10007

ISBN 978-0-06-279775-9
Library of Congress Control Number: 2017947262
Printed and bound in China
First Printing, 2018

Waterproof Cover & Detachable Practice Rope

marine KNOTS

HOW TO TIE 40 ESSENTIAL KNOTS

Patrick Moreau
Illustrations by Jean-Benoît Héron

HARPER DESIGN

An Imprint of HarperCollinsPublishers

contents

◎ eyes and closed loops

These loops are generally divided into two categories:

1) Sliding eyes close around the object to which they are tied.

2) Non-sliding eyes are used more frequently by sailors because they are much easier to untie. There are many types of non-sliding eyes.

◎ eyes and loops in the middle of a rope

These knots allow you to have a fixation point in the middle of a rope, even if you don't have access to the ends, while still respecting the integrity of the rope in terms of traction.

◎ bend knots

A bend knot is used to join two pieces of rope. The most common type joins the two laces of a shoe using a square knot and tying the ends with a bow so that you can immediately untie it.

◎ longitudinal tension knots

When on board we often need to create traction along a rope or even a chain. This happens most often when a sheet jumps out of the winch headstock. Traditionally, we would use a tautline hitch, but there is a very effective alternative that is much easier to untie.

◉ whipping knots

To keep the end of a rope from unraveling, you can solder it, but since the inner and outer materials are different, they will quickly detach from each other. The most efficient solution, of course, is to encase the end in such a way that the strings are pulled together as tightly as possible.

◉ symbolic knots

Finally, here are two knots that make a nice pair. They are not "useful" in the strict sense, since their value lies elsewhere. They are simply quite elegant and sailors wanted to give a name to their creations.

introduction

The art of knot tying is a type of geometry resulting from careful construction, based on logical and, above all, consistent principles. Studying this art only through rote memorization would be very limiting. Unless you use a particular knot regularly, it will quickly be forgotten, which is why we are interested in understanding how they are constructed in order to memorize them more easily.

To construct knots, we will use very specific language based on the following elements.

Logically, every knot starts with an initial hand movement. Since a majority of the population are right-handed, we have decided that the left hand will be the holding hand and the right hand, the working hand. Left-handed users will need to reverse the instructions so that the knot will be created by the left hand as the working hand. The standing end, which is generally the longest part, is located on the underside of the knot and does not move. The right hand crosses the working end—which will create the knot—over the standing end.

The gesture that we will use for the majority of the knots should be simple and flexible, and it should follow the natural curve, which should be clockwise.

If we direct the rope in this way to the right, it will take the form of a curve, which will end by passing over itself to create the first cross.

By starting with this initial gesture and understanding that it is the basis for all simple knots, the learning process becomes easier.

In other words, the simplest way to start is to bring the working end over the standing end.

Before we continue, we should specify a few of the basic principles that will allow you to organize the rope's path to create logical and consistent knots.

As soon as a cross is created, four parts are automatically established that come from the center of the crossing.

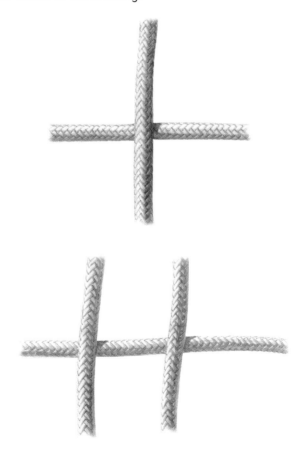

Each part will be interpreted in one of two ways:
  • parallel, solely for creating a braid structure for a complex knot;

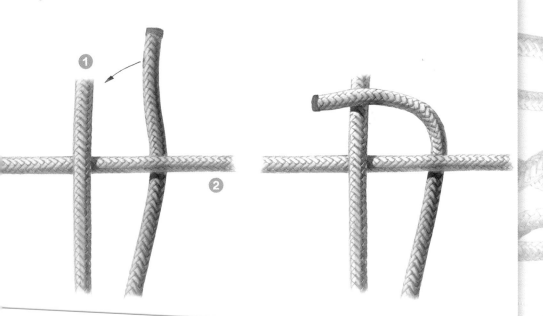

• perpendicular to the center, which applies to direct knots, the ones of most interest to us. The working end is led under part 2 and over part 1.

And thus we have the alternating over-under principle.

the half knot, or simple knot

This is the simplest, most straightforward knot and the one that everyone knows.

Start with the basic opening movement.

Then simply use the loop that you have just created and apply the over-under-over logic.

This creates a half knot, or a simple knot, that will kick off our first category of knots, the stopper knots.

figure-eight knot

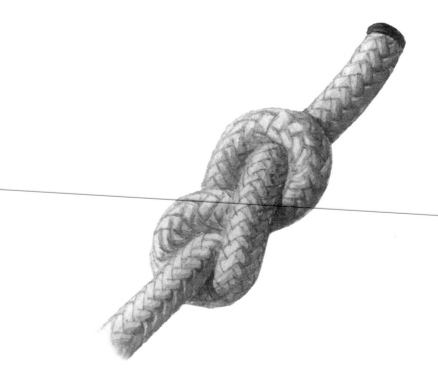

The figure-eight knot is an improvement on the half knot. It is commonly used to keep a sheet from coming out of a fairlead or a pulley. Even after strenuous use, this knot can still be untied. This is why it is the basic knot sailors use to secure a rope.

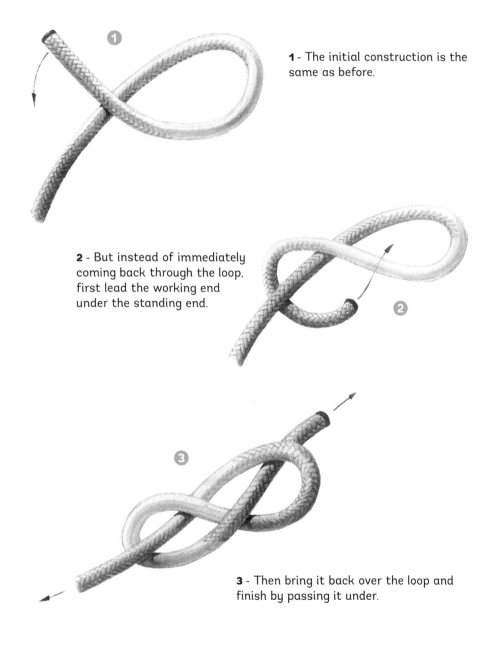

1 - The initial construction is the same as before.

2 - But instead of immediately coming back through the loop, first lead the working end under the standing end.

3 - Then bring it back over the loop and finish by passing it under.

blood knot

If you need a stopper knot that can act as a handle, you can use the blood knot with multiple coils.

Unfairly obscure, this tricky knot is very useful on board boats.

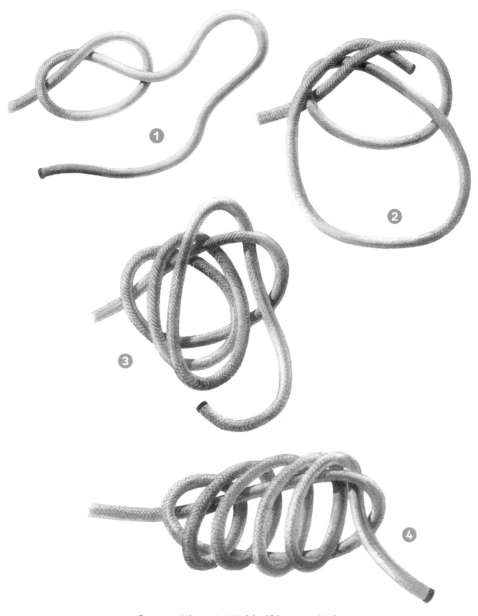

1, 2, 3, and 4 - Start with an initial half knot, which you will then double, triple, quadruple, etc.

5 and 6 - Then start to tighten it down by gently pulling on the two ends until you obtain the construction that looks like a long sideways bight that will be inserted inside the knot.

Next, slide it to the right until it lays against the first half knot.

7 and 8 - Now being careful to stay to the left of the coils you created, make sure that the bight goes into the coils all the way to the left side of the construction.

The slack created by the extra rope will be eliminated by pulling on the working end on the right.

oysterman's stopper knot

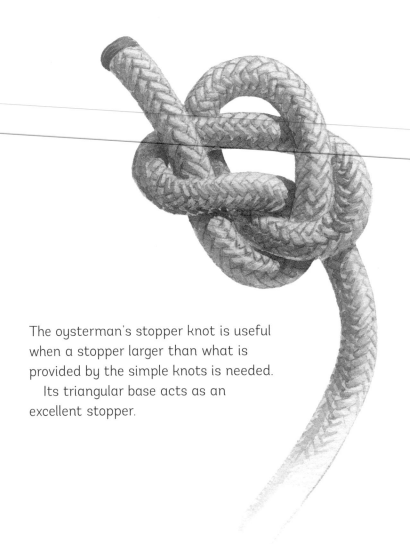

The oysterman's stopper knot is useful when a stopper larger than what is provided by the simple knots is needed. Its triangular base acts as an excellent stopper.

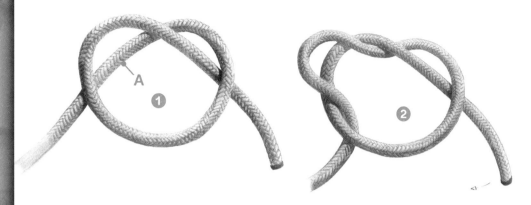

1 and 2 - By once again using the same starting movement, first lead the working end twice over and then under to create an "A" bight twice-under, which you can pull out the top.

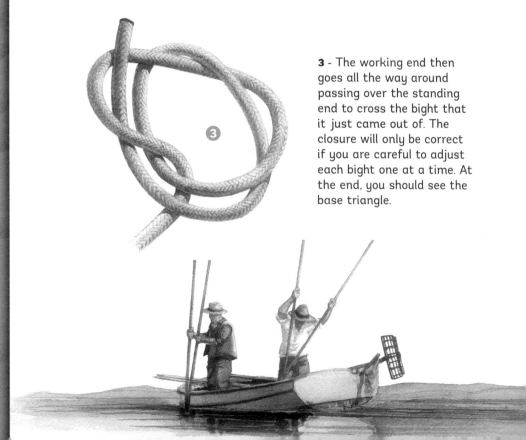

3 - The working end then goes all the way around passing over the standing end to cross the bight that it just came out of. The closure will only be correct if you are careful to adjust each bight one at a time. At the end, you should see the base triangle.

round turn and two half hitches

The value of the round turn cannot be overstated.

While it is quite simple, it allows you to maintain the tension on a rope by increasing arm force. And if the tension is too great, there is nothing wrong with doing a second round turn.

This gesture has somewhat fallen out of favor with pleasure boaters, but it is the first step of the most iconic sailing knot: a round turn and two half hitches.

An exceptional hitching knot, it is one of the few that can be tied and untied under great tension.

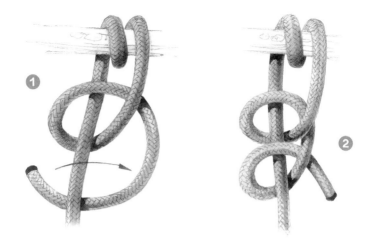

1 and 2 - It is essential that the two half hitches are always knotted in the same direction.

If, as in the diagrams, you tie the first one by first passing the working end under the fixed standing end, you must tie the second one by first passing under.

Of course, there is no reason that you cannot start with the working end passing over, as long as you knot the second one over, too.

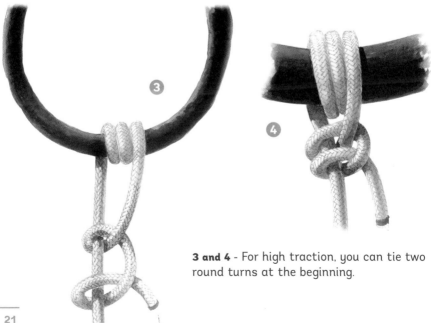

3 and 4 - For high traction, you can tie two round turns at the beginning.

anchor bend

Fairly similar to the round turn and two half hitches, the anchor bend is an excellent hitching knot. It is simple and always very easy to untie, particularly when it has a bight. Originally, it was primarily used to attach a small anchor directly to its buoy rope.

1 - Start with the same movement as for a round turn and two half hitches, but leave a fairly large space between the hitching object and the round turn.

2 - This space should allow the working end to pass through.

In spite of its simplicity, this knot holds very tightly and will not slide.

And once the tension is released, it becomes easy to untie.

3 - Of course, by replacing the end of the rope with a bight, it can be immediately released.

lighterman's hitch

This is another example of the effectiveness of the round turn.

If you have to hitch with a thick rope or if you are mooring a vessel that has a tendency to drift, this knot should be tied. It is often used by boaters to moor a barge.

The secret of this knot is that it is not really a knot. It is held by the round turns and the tension on the end of the rope.

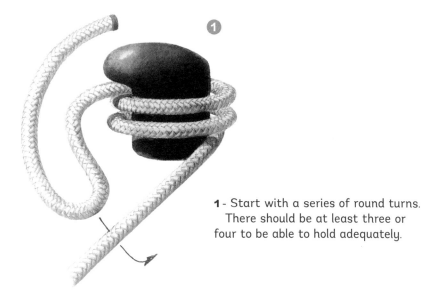

1 - Start with a series of round turns. There should be at least three or four to be able to hold adequately.

2 - Then, using the working end, create a bight that is large enough to go over the hitching object.

This bight is adjusted under tension.

Then you can pull the remaining end over a cleat or tie it up without a knot on a nearby object.

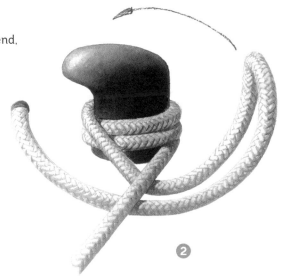

clove hitch

This knot consists of two wrapped half hitches.
 It is an extremely simple and handy knot, making it one of the most popular.
 However, if there is a lot of tension on the rope, it may get stuck and be impossible to untie.

1 - Using a vertical support with an accessible top, the working end passes under the standing end.

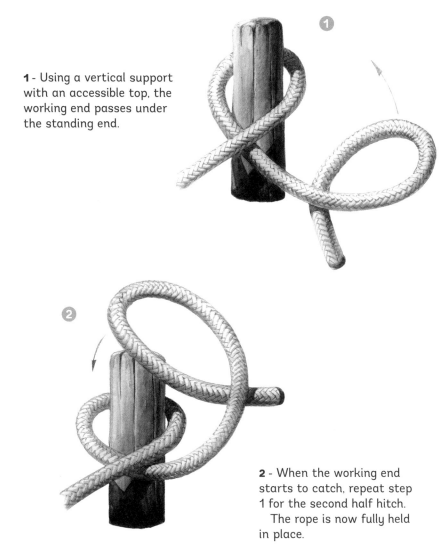

2 - When the working end starts to catch, repeat step 1 for the second half hitch.
The rope is now fully held in place.

constrictor knot

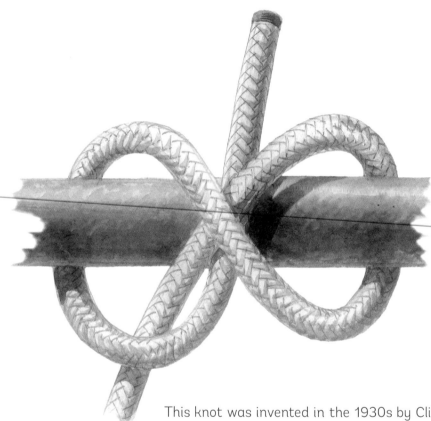

This knot was invented in the 1930s by Clifford Ashley, the author of *The Ashley Book of Knots*.

Its defining feature, compared to the clove hitch, on which it is based, comes from the fact that the two half hitches do not work one after the other, but together.

The constrictor knot is much more effective than the clove hitch and will not come undone.

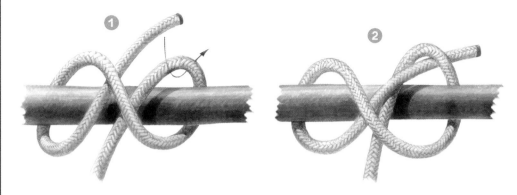

1 and 2 - Rather than continuing with our step-by-step instructions, in this case it is faster and easier to think of it this way: over the standing end and under the cross.

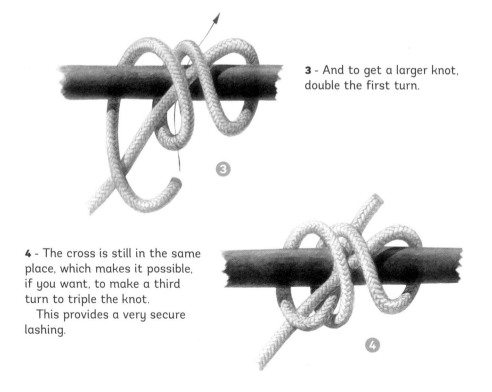

3 - And to get a larger knot, double the first turn.

4 - The cross is still in the same place, which makes it possible, if you want, to make a third turn to triple the knot.

   This provides a very secure lashing.

cow hitch

These two opposing half hitches
are called the cow hitch.

Anyone who is up on their sailing basics
knows this knot, even if they do not know the name.

This elegant and discreet hitch is primarily used to hold an object
with the middle of the rope.

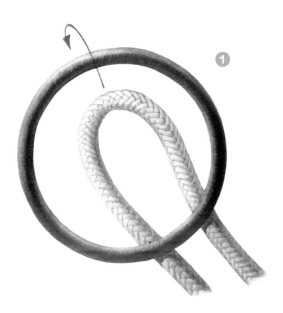

1 and 2 - You simply need to hold the object while separating the two parts of the rope. It is also possible to tie it with a single strand by flipping the second half hitch.

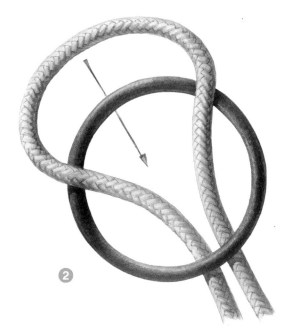

fisherman's bend

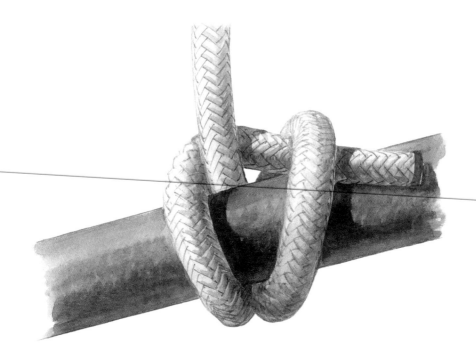

This is a very old knot that has unfortunately fallen into obscurity. It is particularly useful because it does exactly what we expect: reduces the space between the knot and the support.

To hoist a spar whose halyard passes through a pulley or a simple sheave in the mast (like a pole or topsail sprit), using a knot that that is not bulky, the fisherman's bend is ideal.

It is safe, compact, and easy to untie as soon as the tension on the halyard is released.

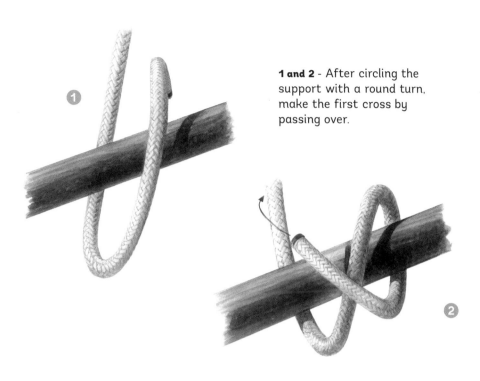

1 and 2 - After circling the support with a round turn, make the first cross by passing over.

3 - Continue to the standing end by passing under, over, then under again in the opposite direction.

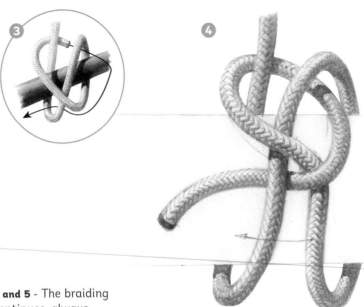

4 and 5 - The braiding continues, always alternating over then under, to create the three-level braid.

If desired, you can continue by creating a bight twice-over followed by a bight twice-under.

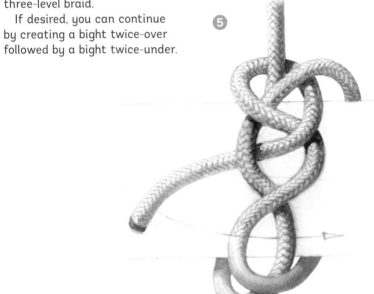

6 - Now that the preparation is finished, we can use it.

The working end is led over the bight twice-over and under the one that is twice under.

This braid ensures that it will hold.

When there is no longer any tension on the knot, after taking in the sails, it can be easily untied.

overhand loop

The simplest sliding eye is the overhand loop, which has been around since the dawn of time.

It can be tied directly with the bight because it is a half knot created just with the bight.

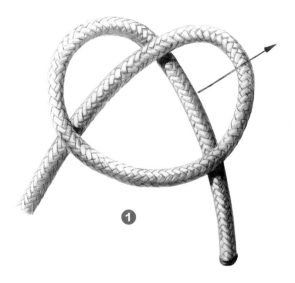

1 and 2 - The first movement is to make a half knot, like before.

The working end passes over, then twice under the right bight, so that it creates a bight twice-under that just needs to be pulled up, like with the half knot.

Tied like this, it can only be used as a temporary stop.

It gets much more interesting when tied around a support (see the noose knot below).

noose knot

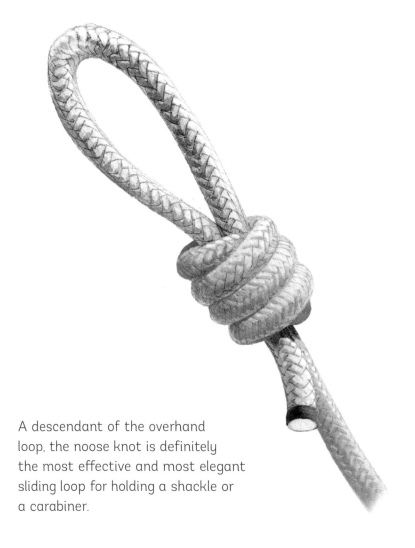

A descendant of the overhand loop, the noose knot is definitely the most effective and most elegant sliding loop for holding a shackle or a carabiner.

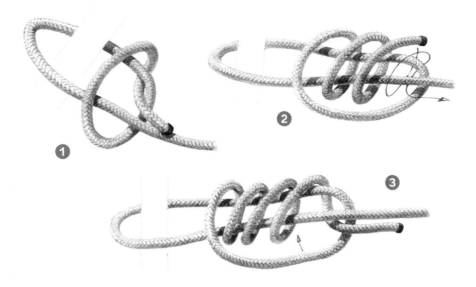

1, 2, and 3 - After leading the rope around the support, tie a half knot at the end of the working end while circling it around the standing end, as if you wanted to encase this end.

And this is exactly what we will do by doubling, tripling, quadrupling the starting half knot.

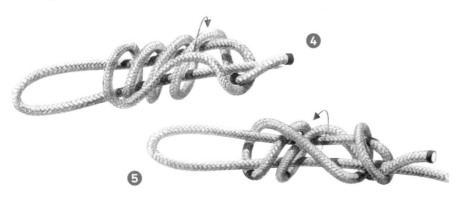

4 and 5 - After tightening a bit from the ends, lead the large sideways bight to the right so that it sits on the starting half knot.

Continue to turn it to the left by carefully inserting it inside the coils, just like for the blood knot, which is the forerunner of the noose knot.

sliding figure-eight knot

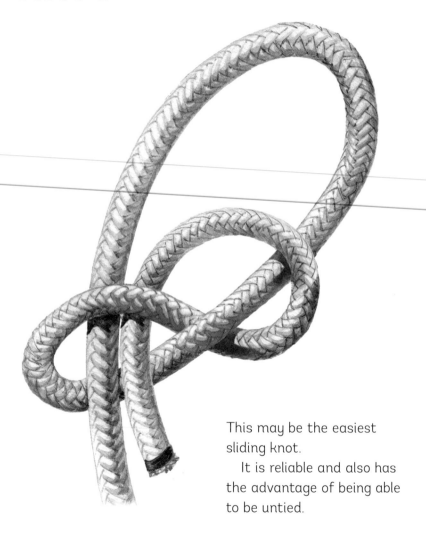

This may be the easiest sliding knot.

It is reliable and also has the advantage of being able to be untied.

1 - Starting with the standing end (the longest part), lead the working end around the support.

2 - A figure-eight knot is created on the standing end, while carefully respecting the alternating under, over, under pattern.

bowline knot

This is the most well-known non-sliding eye, which sailors regularly use because it is effective in various situations.

It was originally used primarily for controlling tension on sheets of square sails.

Later it was used to caulk hulls.

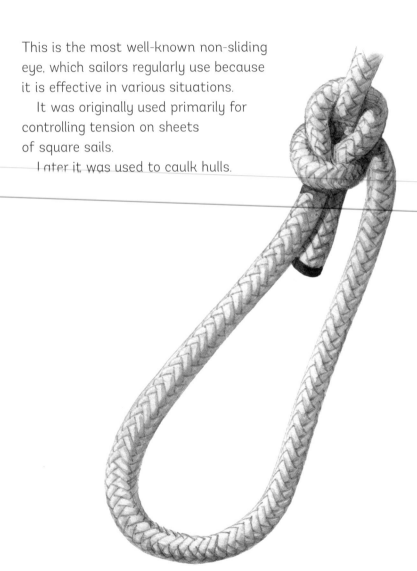

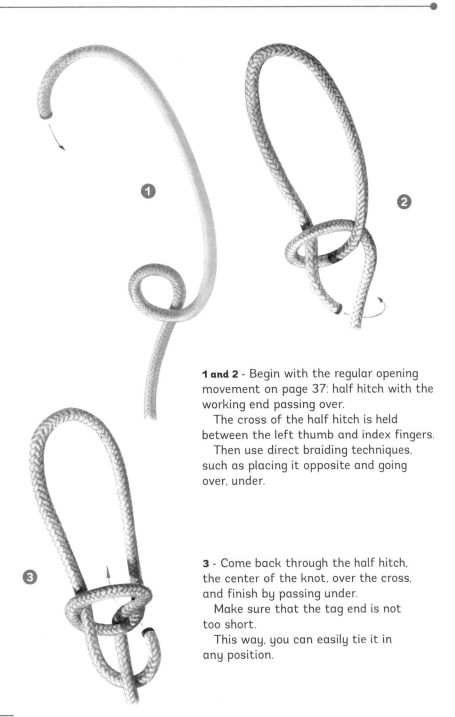

1 and 2 - Begin with the regular opening movement on page 37: half hitch with the working end passing over.

The cross of the half hitch is held between the left thumb and index fingers.

Then use direct braiding techniques, such as placing it opposite and going over, under.

3 - Come back through the half hitch, the center of the knot, over the cross, and finish by passing under.

Make sure that the tag end is not too short.

This way, you can easily tie it in any position.

bowline with a backup knot

Sometimes, if the bowline knot will rub on the ground or another surface, you need to secure it.

The bowline with a backup knot is much more effective than the half hitches that are sometimes added.

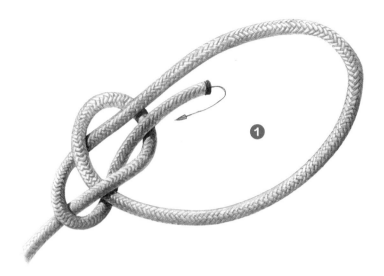

1 and 2 - After coming back through the knot, insert the tag end, which was left a little bit long, inside the knot in the same direction as the standing end.

It will untie just as easily as the basic version.

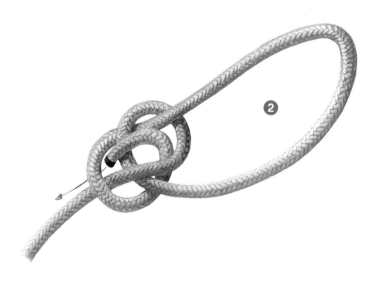

bowline with two successive half hitches

If the knot will be under considerable stress, you can decrease the tension on it by adding a half hitch at the beginning.

This way, the stress will be distributed between the two half hitches.

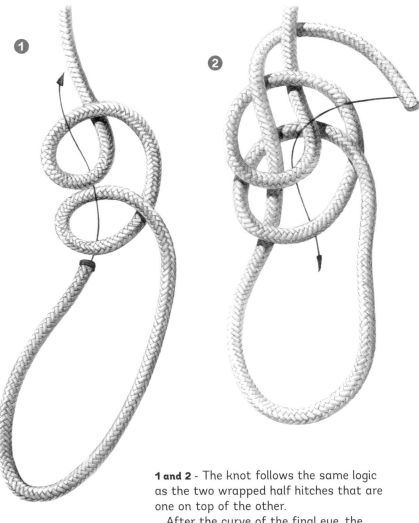

1 and 2 - The knot follows the same logic as the two wrapped half hitches that are one on top of the other.

After the curve of the final eye, the working end comes back over the cross to finish under, with the long part of the strand creating the eye.

portuguese bowline

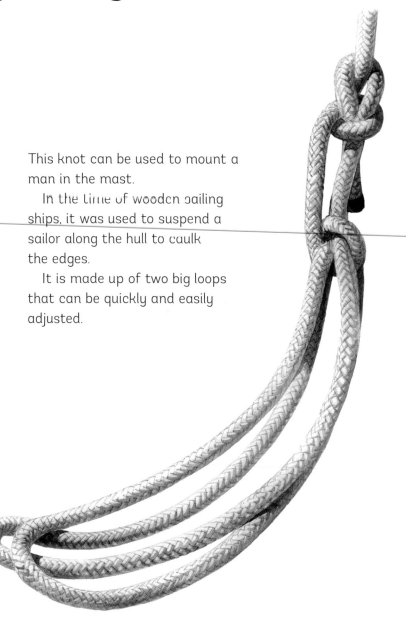

This knot can be used to mount a man in the mast.

In the time of wooden sailing ships, it was used to suspend a sailor along the hull to caulk the edges.

It is made up of two big loops that can be quickly and easily adjusted.

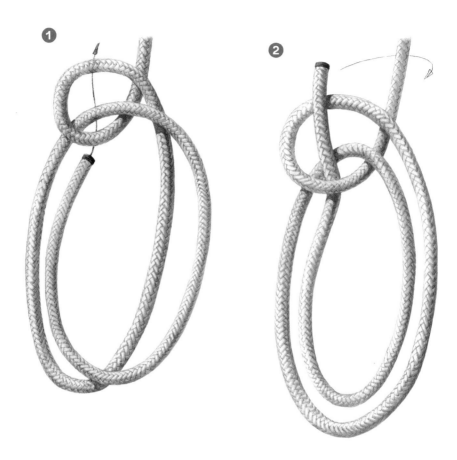

1 and 2 - The regular non-sliding closed loop opening movement is used, working end passing over.

The two loops are created by passing through the half hitch twice, then under and twice over, since there are two loops.

3 - Then create a second half hitch over, in which the working end will pass under, over, etc.

4 - Then you simply finish the bowline on this upper half hitch.

At this point, it can be secured.

5 - The size of the loops (one for the upper leg and the other for the lower back) can be adjusted using the part sliding through the half hitch.

   This isn't the most comfortable means of transportation, but it provides good balance.

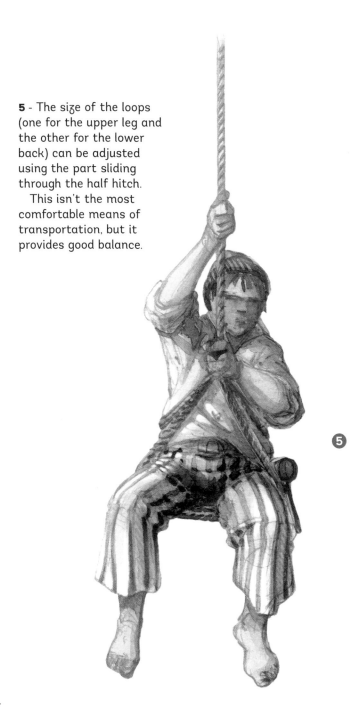

⑤

running bowline knot

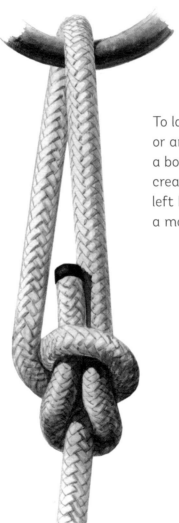

To latch on to a ring, bar, or any other support with a bowline knot, rather than creating a half hitch in the left hand, it can be done in a more free-form way.

A

1 and 2 - Begin by tying a half hitch in the standing end, working end passing over.

Then transfer this half hitch to pass over the standing end.

This is achieved by pulling on the working end at the same time that you push the A-shaped standing end in the opposite direction.

3 - The half hitch has changed places.

Lead the working end under and come back through the half hitch by passing over to finish by passing under.

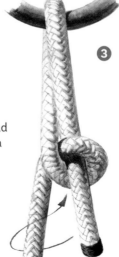

bowline harness knot

Sometimes, in an emergency, you may need to create a hitch that will safely keep you attached to the boat—in other words, a hitch that would act as a harness, without having to go to the trouble of assembling a safety harness.

1 - Using an onboard rope (if possible at least a 14 mm one), place it on your shoulders and neck so that the end held by your right hand just touches the ground to make sure the rope is the right length.

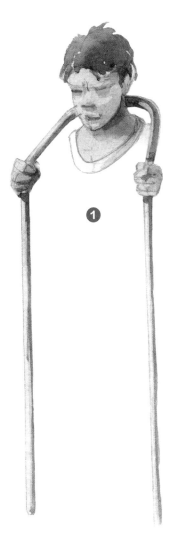

2 - Next lead the two parts to each side of the neck, down the back, adding a twist so that they cross.

Then bring the two ends around to the front and then you just have to tie the bowline knot as close to you as possible.

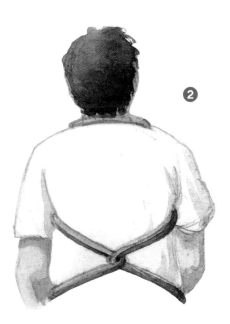

sylvain knot

A young knot enthusiast perfected a non-sliding eye, which leaves nothing to chance and is the result of careful reflection.

The Sylvain knot is easy to untie and to braid, and is excellent for jib sheets.

1 - The working end, which is passed over when the initial half hitch is created, continues on its path passing over, then under and over.

At this point, the knot is basically completed, and though it is quite simple, it can be used as is.

Tension can be applied to the knot as long as the standing end is tight!

As soon as the tension is released, it will come undone by itself.

2 - Of course, the true value of this knot is revealed when it can also stay intact after the tension is released.

To do this, the construction that we have just created must be locked into place.

The working end simply needs to be led under the whole structure and it should parallel the same path as the final eye.

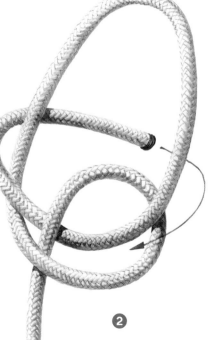

matthew walker knot with one strand

If you need to create a non-sliding eye with a very slippery material like pure Dyneema, the bowline knot may slide. So in this case a special knot is used: the Matthew Walker knot. While it is generally tied with several strands, it can also be done with one eye, with the equivalent of a second strand, which is tied in the first half knot.

Originally, this knot was used to start the crease in the deadeyes, which, with their three holes, allowed the shrouds to be stretched and straightened.

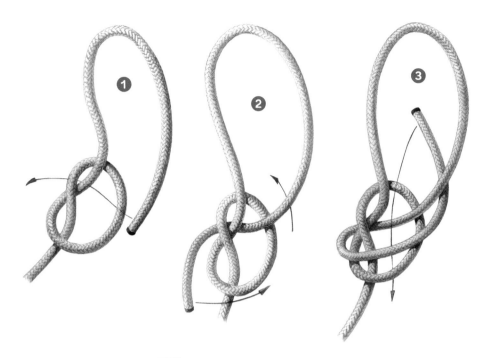

1, 2, and 3 - The two half knots are now intertwined.

4 - The final adjustment must be handled very carefully.

    The best way to do this is to use your right hand to pull on each of the four parts, one at a time, while keeping the structure in your left hand.

    By pushing each pair of the two strands located on either side of the knot, it can be untied fairly easily.

middleman's knot

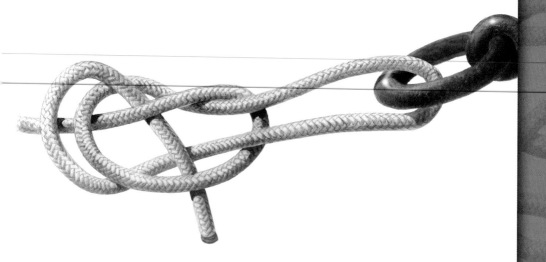

This is a particularly safe loop, which provides excellent hold, even with a stiff nylon line.

It is a classic fish hook knot, preferred by line fisherman over the bowline knot.

The loop can be tied directly in the middle of a rope, but the version using the end of the rope is much more useful because you can pass the string through the eye.

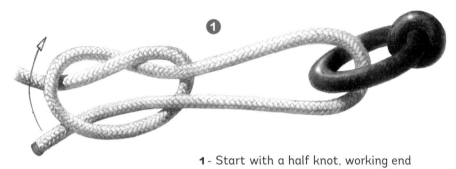

1 - Start with a half knot, working end passing over.

   After inserting the working end in the eye, come back through the half knot in the same place.

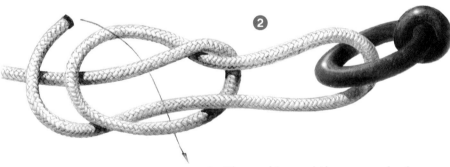

2 - The working end then comes back over the standing end and the first strand of the half knot.

   Then it completes its path by resting in the "V" of the first half knot.

bottle sling knot

This knot, which was invented by a sailing genius, may be the most important knot aboard a ship. It allows you to chill an excellent bottle with complete peace of mind and with admirable elegance.

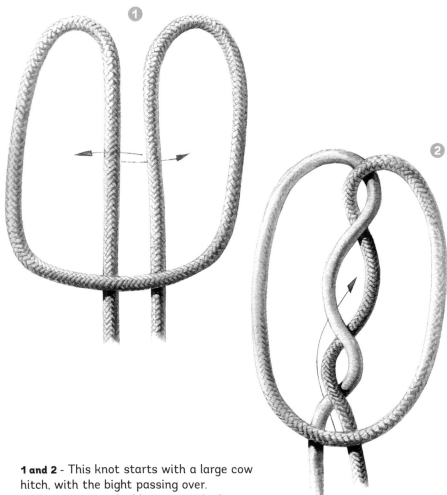

1 and 2 - This knot starts with a large cow hitch, with the bight passing over.

Then create a double twist with the two stands from the middle, while carefully keeping the small bight twice-over located all the way at the bottom of the construction.

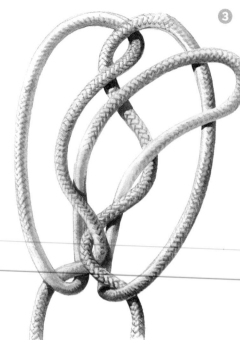

3 and 4 - Now pull on this small bight and lead it to the right so that it comes out passing over.

Finish by shaping the construction to leave the large bight on the right, which you will pass all the way under the structure as indicated by the arrow.

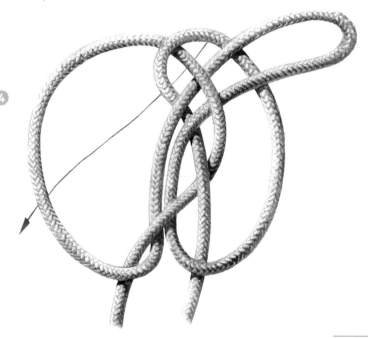

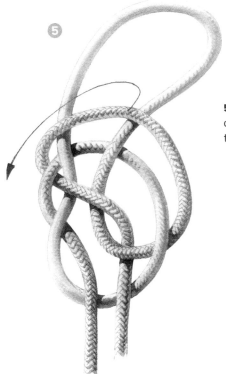

5 - Finally, lead the large upper bight over the whole structure all the way to the bottom of the construction.

6 - The knot is finished.

The neck of the bottle can rest in the space formed by the hexagon, which, with traction, will act like a vice and hold it without any worry that it will slide out.

Then you simply need to pass one of the two ends through the large bight and tie a bend knot with the other end.

This way, it will automatically adjust to suspend the bottle in complete safety.

harness knot

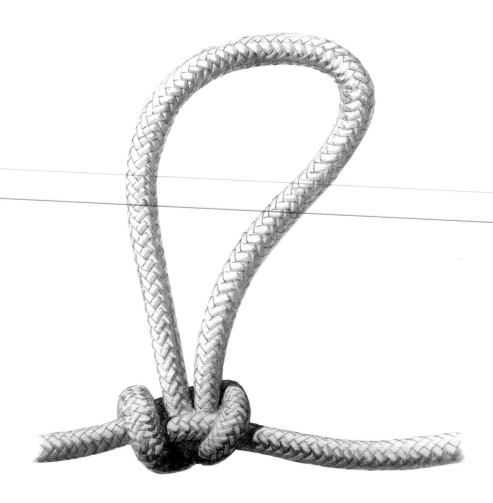

In the past this was called the artillery harness knot. It allowed for the quick creation of an efficient loop to tow cannons. If the traction on the eye is applied at a right angle to the rope, the artillery harness knot is a good choice.

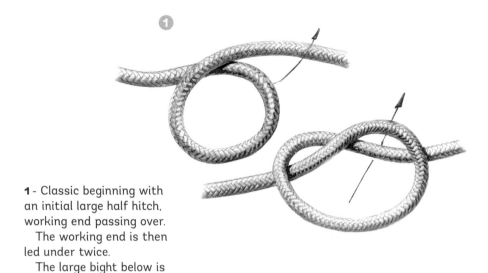

1 - Classic beginning with an initial large half hitch, working end passing over.

The working end is then led under twice.

The large bight below is the final eye.

2 - Lead the large bight under the small one, which is located twice under, and finally pass it over.

Adjust it so that the construction is quite compact.

You can also make an additional twist with the bight of the final eye.

This gives you the double harness knot.

alpine butterfly knot

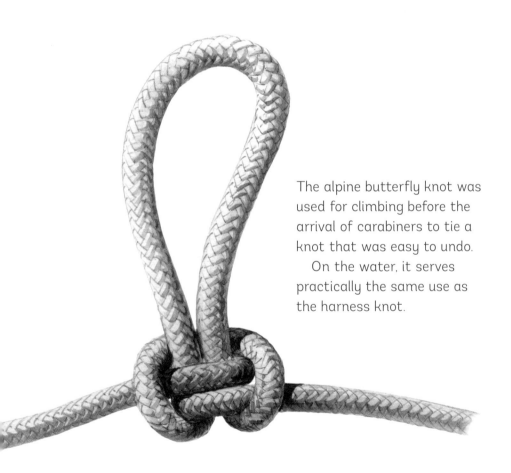

The alpine butterfly knot was used for climbing before the arrival of carabiners to tie a knot that was easy to undo.

On the water, it serves practically the same use as the harness knot.

1 - Create two half hitches one above the other.
   The upper half hitch must be tilted down so that the bight of the lower "A" is clearly seen, twice under.

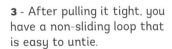

A

2 - Pull this bight from the bottom to the top with your right hand while holding all of the lower part in your left hand.

3 - After pulling it tight, you have a non-sliding loop that is easy to untie.

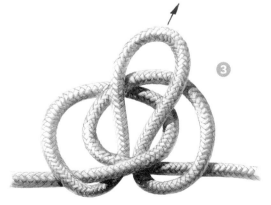

figure-eight traction knot

This knot makes use of the figure-eight knot's various qualities.

It is very useful for landing a halyard using a hoist and it allows you to quickly create an attachment point that is easy to tie and untie even after intense use, without using one of the ends.

There are a wide variety of knots that use the principles of the figure-eight knot.

And this is one of the simplest.

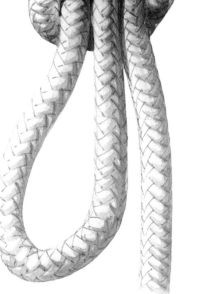

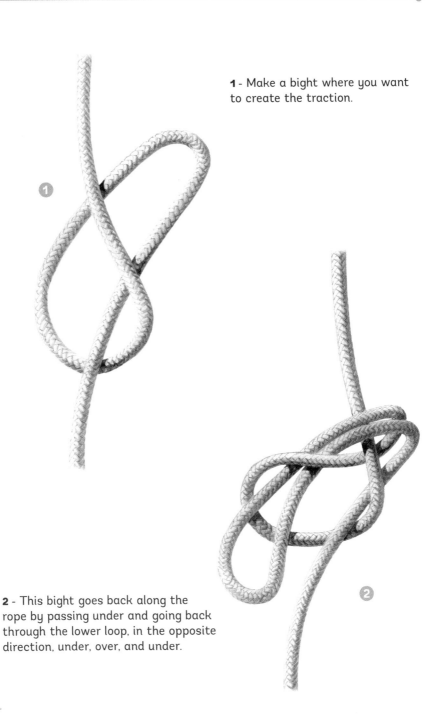

1 - Make a bight where you want to create the traction.

2 - This bight goes back along the rope by passing under and going back through the lower loop, in the opposite direction, under, over, and under.

square knot

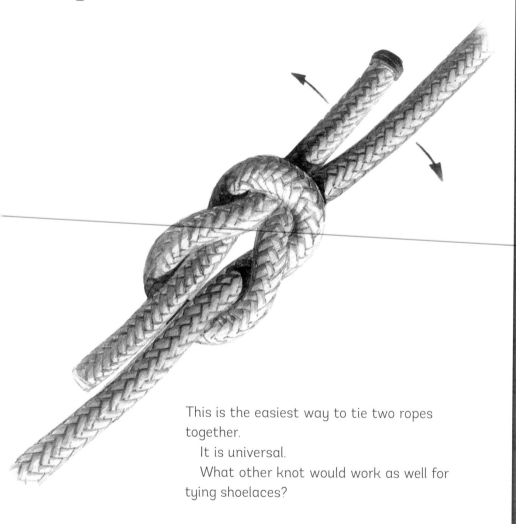

This is the easiest way to tie two ropes together.

It is universal.

What other knot would work as well for tying shoelaces?

1 and 2 - The square knot always starts with a first cross, then a twist of the two parts.

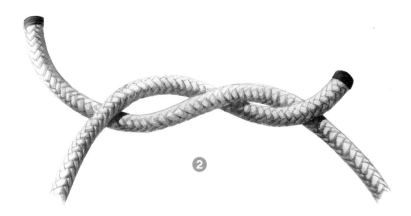

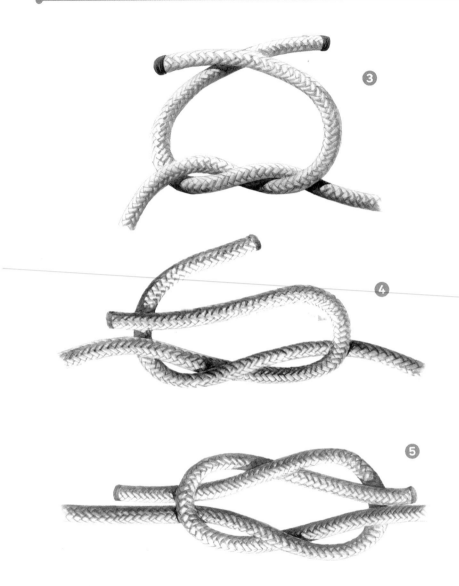

3, 4, and 5 - The left strand starts and finishes its path by passing over. It will complete all of the other crosses by passing over as well.

When the two strands cross again, the right strand returns to the left by passing over, then under, then finishes its path passing over.

After strong traction has been applied, to easily untie it, pull on the two strands located on the same side but opposite each other.

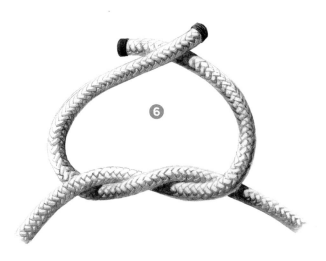

6 and 7 - Lots of people tie a cow hitch instead of a square knot and do not understand why their laces do not stay tied.

   The difference is small but essential.

   When they are tied this way, the strands will only slide.

updated square knot with a bight

Even though it does not have a marine application, how can we ignore the only knot that everyone uses in daily life?

To tie shoelaces, and then easily untie them, you just have to create two bights on one or both of the two ends during the second twist of the strands.

1 - The looped right strand will be lead to the left by crossing over the other bight.

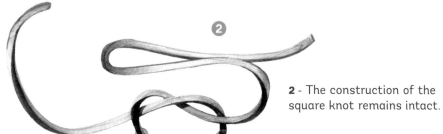

2 - The construction of the square knot remains intact.

3 - With some materials, like leather, especially if it is new and, more particularly, if it has a square section, add a twist using one of the two bights to increase the holding capacity.

   Tied this way, it is truly like a vice.

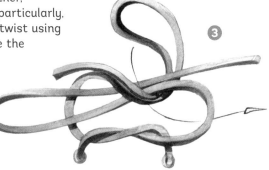

fisherman's knot

Sailors prefer the simplicity of the fisherman's knot for reef points that are small in diameter, especially if it is a final bend knot.

Here, two half knots are pulled against each other, which prevents any sliding.

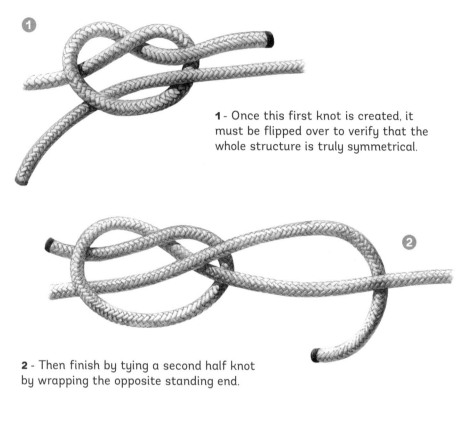

1 - Once this first knot is created, it must be flipped over to verify that the whole structure is truly symmetrical.

2 - Then finish by tying a second half knot by wrapping the opposite standing end.

3 - If you think you may need to untie this bend knot, the two half knots can be replaced by figure-eight knots.

sheet bend

The bend knot most often used by sailors is still the sheet bend and all of its derivations (double sheet bend, triple, Y-shaped, or updated), especially when the two ropes are of different diameters.

It was initially created to regulate tension on sheets.

This use gave it its name, even if today it is used for other applications.

1 - If the ends to be tied are of different sizes, create a loop with the thicker rope.

You can also use an eye that has already been created with a knot or a splice.

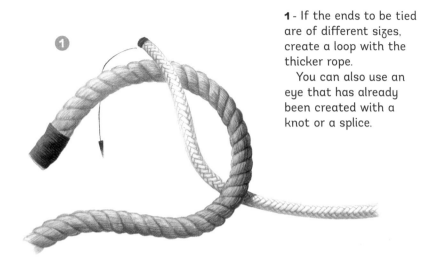

2 - The other strand is led into this loop from bottom to top.

Then it passes under the whole structure to come back and finish its path by being tightened on itself.

3 and 4 - This knot can be doubled for better hold or
a bight can be created so that it can be immediately
released.

5 - You can also create a bend with two elements that are
going to go in different directions, but that are from the same
primary rope.

6 - Finally, if the difference in diameter between the two ropes
is significant, you can improve the sheet bend by adding a
holding point.
   The working end returns from the back on and under itself.

carrick bend

Some say that Saint Carrick, an Irish monk who lived in the Middle Ages, is the patron saint of topmen because it is with his knot that we create the safest bend between two ropes: the Carrick bend.

This knot is also interesting because it is the gateway to advanced seamanship, since it requires a preparation that we will use for braiding.

Finally, no matter what the tension placed on the knot, you can always untie it relatively easily.

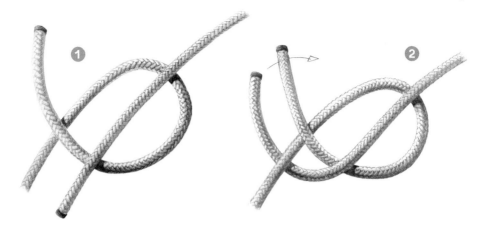

1 and 2 - If the half hitch of the left rope started by passing over, the second rope will be led to its first half hitch twice over in the same direction as the standing end of the left rope.

The preparation is finished now and you can braid with the right rope, which is opposite, with the part of the first rope passing under.

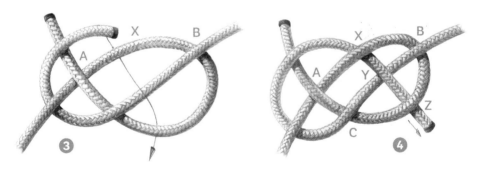

3 and 4 - The path is still in opposition but now with that part continuing over.

To pass under, choose the bight twice-under, indicated by A B which is closest.

You have just used the main rule of braiding:

Bight twice-under, I go under.

Bight twice-over, I go over.

After the braiding, you simply continue with consistent bights, over at one cross, under at the next, for example XA and XB, YC and YB, ZC and ZB.

In this way, the structure is certain to hold tight.

When this is put into use, the strands may slide a bit, but they will quickly lock into a very compact knot. Even after being used for an extended period under pressure, it can always be untied.

bosun's whistle knot

The Carrick bend is the starting point for a number of knots, including the bosun's whistle knot, which is definitely the best button that you can create with your hands.

In the era of sailing ships, bosuns used this knot to tie their famous whistle around their neck, which they used to give orders from the mast.

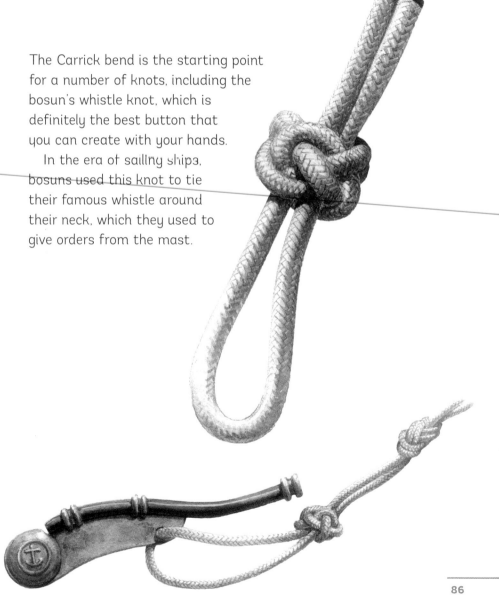

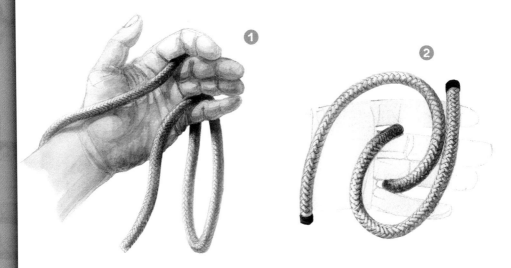

1 and 2 - First step: the two strands pass between your fingers and turn around each other to the left without crossing.

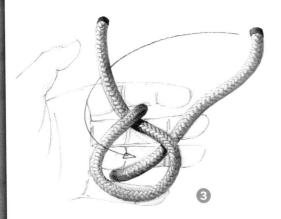

3 - After leading the right strand under itself to its starting point, lead the lower strand in the same way: under, over, and under itself.

4 - The Carrick knot is tied flat. The two tag ends are diagonally opposite each other and go out by passing over.

5 - Since this knot ends up being very thick, begin rounding it off using a finger, preferably the index.

Lead each working end over the standing end opposite it to bring it out in the middle of the knot in a square.

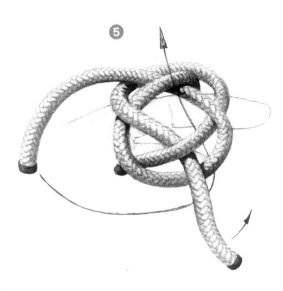

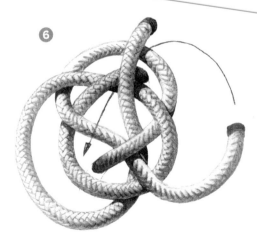

6 - Be careful to respect the rotational direction of the rope by turning it to the left.

The two tag ends are now passed through the middle of the knot.

Hold the whole knot in your left hand and tighten it a bit to hold the strands.

Then pull on each standing end one at a time to tighten them.

7 - Hold the knot tightly in your hand and pull on the two working ends at the same time until you get a button shape.

8 - The tightening must be done with care.
   You must go bight by bight, changing strand with each movement so that it is truly symmetrical and tight, until it is a compact button.

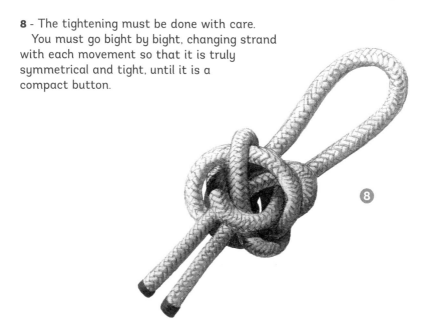

button strap knot

This is a knot that sailors have been using since the dawn of time.

Using the button strap knot, you can grab any rope, moor objects, a sheet, etc. Just before tying the bosun's whistle knot to make a button, tie a simple half knot in the middle of the rope.

1 - When you are ready to use it, if you close it by passing the button through the middle of the half knot, the strap can only be used once: after applying intense traction, it will be almost impossible to untie it.

However, if you switch from a half knot to a half hitch, just by pulling on one of the two bights of the half knot, you can pass the button through the eye that was created and then reclose the strap.

Even after intense use, it will always be easy to untie.

locked button strap knot

The perfect button strap knot will allow the rope to keep all of its integrity without shearing.

In order to do this, you need a particular kind of rope with extensible braiding into which the rope can be inserted.

Because of its high performance in terms of resistance to breaks, we recommend a pure Dyneema fiber braid.

This requires the use of an open needle like the one shown on the next page.

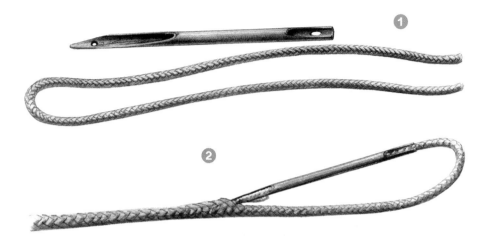

1 and 2 - After threading the end of the braid through the eye of the open needle, determine the size of the eye for the buttonhole and lead it through the braid to the right place for the desired length.

3 - After you lead the needle out of the braid, you will have the two strands that will be used to create the bosun's whistle knot button.

Ideally, the size of the closed eye should be smaller than the button.

Just slide the eye open and pass the button through before reclosing the eye, by sliding it again.

klemheist knot

If you are going to apply longitudinal tension along a stretched rope or rigid bar without being able to create any attachment point, then a Klemheist knot should be used. This knot is commonly employed by climbers.

In these two variations, it is one of the most recent and certainly one of the smartest ways to apply traction along an axis.

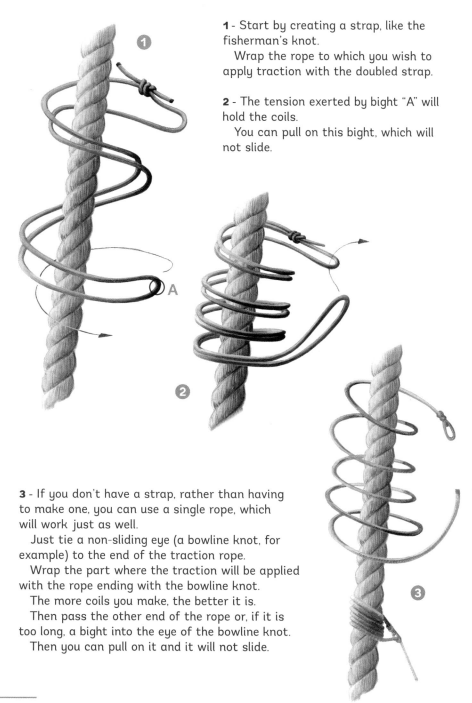

1 - Start by creating a strap, like the fisherman's knot.

Wrap the rope to which you wish to apply traction with the doubled strap.

2 - The tension exerted by bight "A" will hold the coils.

You can pull on this bight, which will not slide.

3 - If you don't have a strap, rather than having to make one, you can use a single rope, which will work just as well.

Just tie a non-sliding eye (a bowline knot, for example) to the end of the traction rope.

Wrap the part where the traction will be applied with the rope ending with the bowline knot.

The more coils you make, the better it is.

Then pass the other end of the rope or, if it is too long, a bight into the eye of the bowline knot.

Then you can pull on it and it will not slide.

circus hitch

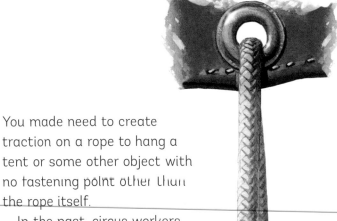

You made need to create traction on a rope to hang a tent or some other object with no fastening point other than the rope itself.

In the past, circus workers used this knot exclusively to tie the thin ropes used to secure the tents.

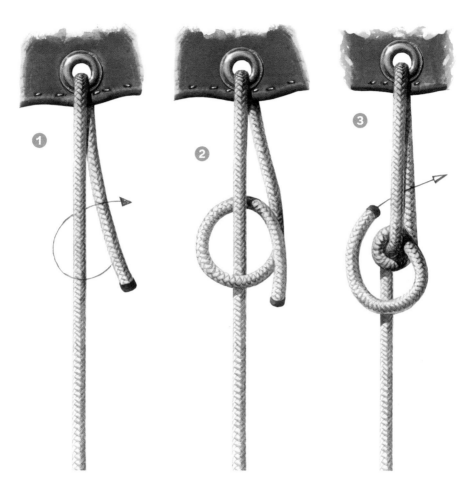

1 and 2 - The rope passes through the ring of the object to be hung.
   When coming back through, create a half hitch on the standing end,
with the working end passing over.

3 - After applying as much tension as possible by lowering the half
hitch all the way down along the standing end, lead the working end
under the half hitch so that it starts to come through the coil.
   Then lead it up.
   Once it is in this position, pull on the working end as hard as possible.
   The rope should lock between the two strands while creating an
elbow on the lower part of the eye which will prevent any sliding.
   Then you just need to fasten it with a half hitch tied under.

long whipping knot

When working with a longer piece of rope, in order to keep the binding tight, use a long whipping knot that doesn't have length limitations.

Aside from the blood knot, no other knot is tighter, even stitched whipping.

1 - Start with very tight round turns with the long part of the sail rope, while also holding the end of the same rope.

Continue until about half of the final length is covered, then insert a marlinspike for the rest of the sheathing.

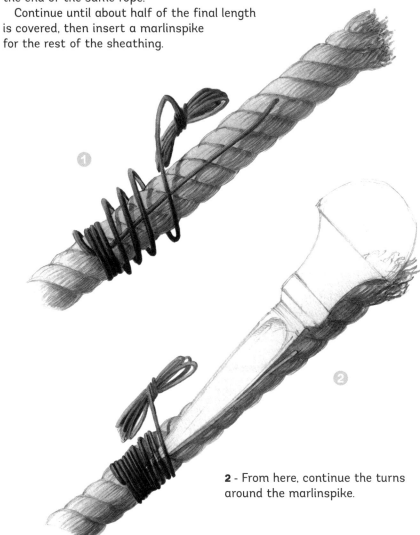

2 - From here, continue the turns around the marlinspike.

3 - Continue until the entire section
needed is covered and then cut the rope,
keeping enough length to thread the
rope along the marlinspike coming
from behind.

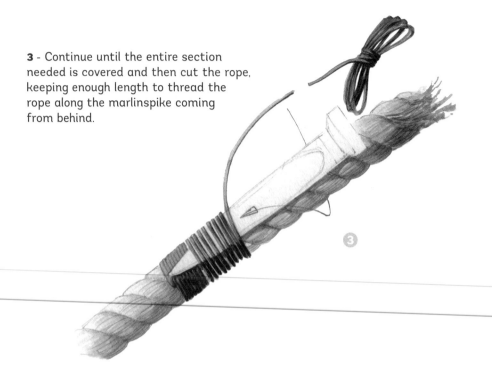

④ - Once the rope is in place, pull out the
marlinspike and begin tightening bight by
bight, starting from point A all the way to
the end, using the point of the marlinspike.
   Then from point G, just pull the part of
the rope that is now coming out of
the middle of the whipping.

A

G

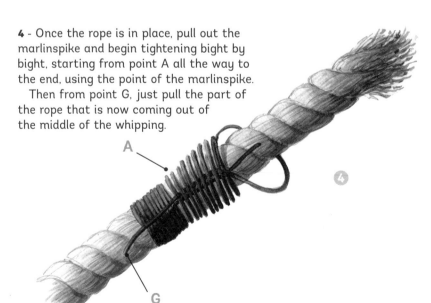

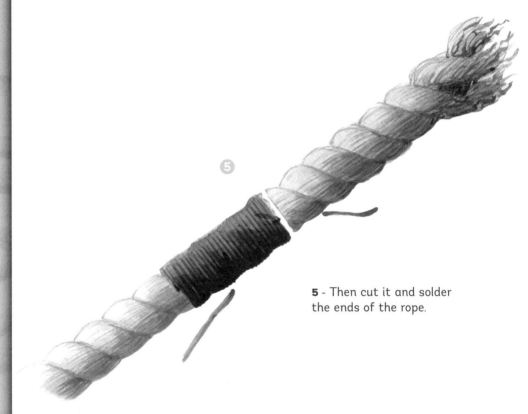

5 - Then cut it and solder the ends of the rope.

whipping with a blood knot

If you want to stop the end of a rope quickly without doing a long whipping, you can use the excellent holding capacities of the blood knot.

But you cannot make more than seven turns: beyond that, the strands end up overlapping, which prevents a tight closure.

1 - Start by creating a half knot with the rope to be whipped, while wrapping it around the rope whose end you want to cover.

2 - Double it by passing twice, and then a third time and finally a fourth, for example.

You can make up to seven turns.

3 - After slightly tightening it using a little bit of traction on the two ends, hold the large sideways bight and lead it to the right, positioning it exactly over the half knot of the base that should be apparent.

Now, elongate this bight between the strands without crossing any of them, while staying to the left of the coils.

Make sure that this bight inserts perfectly between the strands already in place.

4 - After leading the large bight all the way to the left of the construction, create some slack by applying light traction to the right strand.

Now you can tighten it.

Pull on the two ends at the same time, then push or tap on the whipping with the marlinspike so that the coils settle into place.

Finally, pull as hard as you can, with pliers if necessary, to increase the level of force.

Now just cut the ends and solder them.

lover's knot

In the middle of the nineteenth century, in the United States, when a whaler was courting a girl that he was in love with, he gave her a special kind of knot that she had to give back to him.

Depending on how she returned the knot to the whaler, it would convey her feelings toward him.

If the knot was almost undone, the guy didn't have a chance. If she gave it back to him as it was, without tightening or loosening it, it meant that she was just a good friend. However, if she gave the knot back to him tightened with the two little hearts tied together, it meant that she was "spoken for," and that it was time to weigh anchor and spread the news.

Since that time, it has been called the lover's knot.

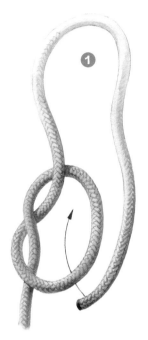

1 - Start with a half knot with the working end passing over going up.

2 - The working end goes down and comes back through the eye of the first half knot to be led over the strand going down.

3 - Before finishing the second half knot under, over.

sailor's cross knot

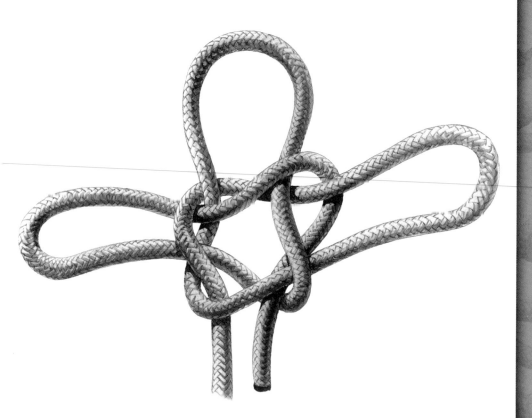

Starting with the lover's knot, you can create
a very elegant forestay in the middle of a rope
called the sailor's cross knot.

This knot, along with the triskelion, is one of
the Celtic knot symbols.

1 and 2 - You just have to take the bights in the middle of the knot and bring them out to each side while keeping the integrity of the upper bight.

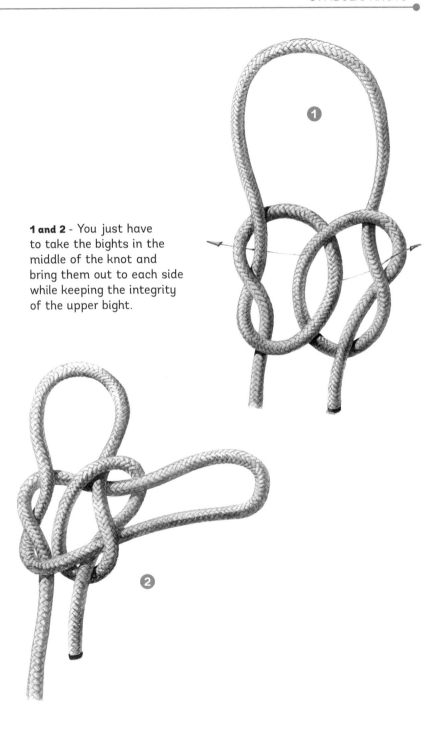

glossary

barge: boat for transporting material pulled on towpaths.

bend: knot that temporarily brings together two ends.

bosun: foreman of the deck crew responsible for the rigging in the era of sailing ships.

buoy rope: thick rope generally used to lengthen the anchor chain.

caulk a hull: fill the space between the planking with caulk to make the hull waterproof.

cleats: pieces of wood or metal around which you can moor a rope.

coils: in a knot, the coils are always made around the hand or a support.

crease: rope that passes through the holes of the deadeye to stretch and land the shrouds and the stays. The crease is the precursor of the turnbuckle.

deadeyes: round pieces of wood with three holes for tightening the creases in the shrouds.

fairlead: allows you to guide the ropes.

gasket: a thin rope, between 2 and 5 mm.

halyards: ropes that allow you to hoist the sails.

hoist: made up of several pulleys and a rope; allows you to increase arm force to pull hard, in other words, to land.

jib: front sail.

landing: placing the most tension possible on a rope or line.

marlinspike: an essential sailing tool; it allows you to open a rope to pull another strand through.

planking: long planks of wood that cover the hull of a boat.

rigging: all of the metal and fabric ropes that are part of a sailboat's equipment.

running rigging: all of the ropes on a boat.

sheave: disk recessed in the inner part of a pulley, which the ropes of a hoist pass over.

sheets: ropes that allow you to adjust the tension on the sails.

shrouds: metal ropes that hold the masts.

spar: piece of wood that makes up the rigging.

splice: two ropes that are linked by tying together the strands.

standing end: part of the rope that is supposedly fixed; starting from the point that you have chosen to create the knot, it is the lower part of the structure. The standing end doesn't move. It is passive.

strap: ring of rope closed by a splice or a bend knot.

tag end: the end of the working end that goes past the knot.

taking in the sails: action of lowering the sails along the mast or a stay.

tight: when a rope is tight it is very stretched out.

topmen: sailors who, in the era of sailing ships, climbed onto the mast.

topsail sprit: piece of wood parallel to the peak on a for-and-aft rig.

working end: the end of rope that creates the knot.

wrapping: wrap a support with a rope.

illustrator

Jean-Benoît Héron is from a family of publishers and illustrators.

Trained as an engineer, he began to work as an illustrator in 1995.

He specialized in architectural drawings, both on land and sea, and exploded-view drawing of monuments, reconstructions, lighthouses, and boats. He regularly works for the National Marine Museum in Paris, the Monte-Carlo Société des Bains de Mer, the medieval construction site at Guédelon Castle, and the National Monuments Center in Paris. He also works with various other publishers.

Héron is the author of *Ces bateaux qui ont découvert le monde* (2013) and the illustrator of *Histoire(s) de phares* (2015).

author

Patrick Moreau's passion for knots was born when he saw an old bosun tying knots and splices on the rigging of his first boat, a small cutter, in the Rade de Brest, France.

After working in various sectors, at the age of fifty, Moreau decided to "get serious" and began working with knots—first on riggings for sailboats, and then by creating training programs about knots.

The magazine *Voiles et voiliers* asked him to write an introductory book that was followed by two more books, and two instructional videos.

Today Moreau, known as Dr. Knot, assists on classic sailboats and organizes maritime internships.

He has dedicated himself to refining the pedagogy of knot tying.